Couples Communication

Strengthening Your Relationship with Effective Dialogue

Table of Contents

Chapter 1. Introduction

Embrace the power of words and understand their impact on your relationship with our Special Report: "Couples Communication: Strengthening Your Relationship with Effective Dialogue". This comprehensive guide, peppered with insights from renowned relationship psychologists, offers game-changing strategies to help you and your partner converse more fluidly, understand each other deeply, and grow closer with every shared word. Whether you're in the sunlit honeymoon phase of your relationship or traversing stormy circumstances, this report is your go-to tool to build bridges not walls, fostering a climate of understanding and mutual respect. Uplifting, practical, and actionable, this Special Report is an investment in your love life that pays dividends in harmony and happiness. Don't miss the opportunity to transform your couple dynamic, build a rock-solid foundation, and ignite a dialogue that both of you deserve. Order your copy today!

Chapter 2. Understanding the Importance of Effective Communication

Many of us underestimate the power of words, believing actions to be the decisive determinant in our relationships. Yet, words can be used to apologize, persuade, heal wounds, encourage, and forge deeper connections, serving as a mirror for our emotions, thoughts, and beliefs. When effectively utilized, communication hones and sharpens the interpersonal dynamic, fostering deeper understanding and intimacy. This idea, central to relationship growth, forms the foundation of this chapter.

2.1. The Power of Words

Words exist as a bridge between two minds, allowing us to share ideas, desires, and emotions. Often, the misunderstandings that plague relationships stem from an inability or reluctance to effectively communicate. The adage "actions speak louder than words" may bear truth, yet this only underscores the importance of being able to articulate verbally what your actions might be expressing or intending.

Being engaged in productive conversation with your partner helps you in multiple ways. It gives you the language to describe your feelings, name your needs, and negotiate solutions to issues before they become intractable problems. It also allows you to appreciate your partner's world, their values, and their aspirations.

Equally, the undervalued art of active listening, an integral component of effective communication, reinforces to the speaker that they are heard, appreciated, and understood.

2.2. The Ripple Effect of Communication Breakdown

In contrast, a lack of effective communication can lead the relationship to stall. Misunderstanding, resentment, and frustration can fester, growing into disputes and even leading to relationship breakdown. Disagreements are inevitable in any relationship, yet without communication skills, navigating through such conflict becomes increasingly challenging.

Moreover, a passion that isn't addressed with open dialogue often manifests in passive-aggressive behaviors or emotional distancing that undermines the relationship's core pillars: trust, respect, and intimacy. In essence, poor communication drains the connection of its positive attributes, eventually leading to dissatisfaction, discontent, and disconnection.

2.3. Active Listening: The Unsung Hero

Active listening involves not merely hearing your partner's words but truly understanding their intended meaning. To do so, engage fully with your partner when they are speaking - no distractions, no forming of responses in your mind in advance. Active listening prompts us to lean in, make eye contact, ask clarifying questions, summarize what you've heard, and empathize with their feelings.

Demonstrating through your behaviors that you genuinely value your partner's thoughts cultivates an environment of mutual respect and understanding. When both parties actively practice this, the communication proficiency within a relationship increases tenfold, thereby leading to a more considerable depth of connection.

2.4. Openness and Honesty: The Path to Authenticity

Not all truths are comfortable to communicate, yet honesty plays a pivotal role in effective dialogue. Often, avoiding uncomfortable topics to spare each other's feelings leaves problems unresolved, making way for resentment to breed.

Being honest about your feelings or concerns is an investment in the relationship's future. It won't always be easy, but courage in conversation paves the path towards authenticity in a relationship. Ensuring you relay your message with love and respect can encourage your partner to do the same, thus creating an open, accepting space for dialogue.

2.5. Constructive Conflict: Growth Through Disagreement

Not all conflict is harmful. Indeed, some disagreements can serve as catalysts for growth. However, for differences to be constructive rather than destructive, effective communication is key. This includes expressing feelings without blame, focusing on the issue rather than personal attacks, finding compromise, and agreeing to disagree if necessary. Remember the goal isn't to win an argument, but to reach a mutually beneficial solution which satisfies both parties involved.

2.6. Practice Makes Perfect

Transforming the way you communicate in your relationship won't happen overnight. It involves patience, practice, and commitment from both parties. While learning a new language of love, you may falter at times, but make sure to celebrate your successes along the way. And remember, the journey is equally crucial as the destination in discovering a new depth of love and understanding with your partner.

In conclusion, the impact of effective communication on the emotional health of a relationship is immense. While it may seem daunting, embracing communication as a life-skill can lead to relationship experiences that are far richer, more understanding, and deeply satisfying. Practicing this art will lead to a level of intimacy where words become bridges, leading to a deeper understanding of your partner and fostering an enduring connection.

Chapter 3. Developing Emotional Intelligence in Conversations

Developing emotional intelligence in conversations is an essential requisite for fostering a deep and meaningful relationship with your partner. It involves not just understanding your own feelings, but also acknowledging and validating your partner's emotions.

3.1. Understanding Emotional Intelligence

Emotional Intelligence (EI) is the ability to identify, understand, and manage emotions to foster productive and effective interpersonal relationships. Daniel Goleman, an American psychologist, developed a model that outlines five components of EI:

1. Self-awareness: Recognizing and understanding our own emotions.

2. Self-regulation: The ability to control impulsive feelings and behaviors, manage emotions healthily, and adapt to change.

3. Internal motivation: A driving ambition that comes from within, not from external rewards.

4. Empathy: Understanding others' feelings and considering their perspective.

5. Social skills: The ability to communicate well with others, manage conflicts, and work well in teams.

This EI model can be efficiently used in your conversations, enabling you both to better understand each other at an emotional level.

3.2. Building Emotional Self-Awareness

Self-awareness is the foundational block of emotional intelligence. It requires careful introspection and a willingness to accept your feelings, whether positive or negative.

1. Mindfulness Practice: To grow mindful, set aside a few quiet moments each day purposefully to focus on your emotions without judgment.

2. Journaling: Write about your day, your feelings, and your reactions. This will help you understand patterns in your emotional responses.

3. Emotional Check-ins: Regularly ask yourself, "How am I feeling right now?" This practice will help you become more aware of your emotional state at any given time.

Make a habit of these practices and soon you'll notice clearer understanding of your own emotional triggers and responses, which is the first step to develop emotional intelligence.

3.3. The Art of Self-Regulation in Conversations

The ability to regulate one's emotions, especially in heated situations, is crucial in maintaining constructive dialogue.

1. Take a Pause: Before reacting to a triggering comment, give yourself a moment to calm down and collect your thoughts.

2. Reword Your Statement: Instead of saying, "You're always late!" say, "I feel stressed when I'm kept waiting. Can we work something out?" Transforming blame into a request fosters positivity.

3. Assertiveness: Convey your feelings and needs clearly without disrespecting or disregarding your partner's needs.

3.4. Embracing Empathy in Communication

Empathy is the ability to understand and share the feelings of your partner.

1. Active Listening: Show interest, ask clarifying questions, and display encouraging non-verbal behaviors. Reflect back on what you've heard to show understanding.

2. Validate Their Feelings: Acknowledge their feelings by saying something like, "I can see how that would make you upset."

3. Share in Their Emotions: Being empathetic sometimes means sharing in your partner's emotions, be it joy, sorrow, or anger.

3.5. Boosting Social Skills Through Conversations

Social skills are all about effective communication, understanding social dynamics, and being comfortable with resolving conflicts.

1. Respectful Dialogue: Each conversation should be a two-way street, where both partners exchange ideas and feelings freely.

2. Conflict Resolution: Use conflict as an opportunity to grow closer by reaching a resolution that respects both partner's needs and wants.

3. Emotional Vocabulary: Learn to articulate your feelings with precision to avoid miscommunication.

By investing time and effort into developing emotional intelligence within your conversations, your relationship can only grow stronger. Embrace the journey together, because every step forward is a step towards a deeper, healthier and more fulfilling relationship. Remember, all great conversations begin with a step towards understanding. Practice these strategies and unleash the power of emotionally intelligent conversations.

Chapter 4. Mastering Active Listening: The Key to Empathy

Active listening forms the bedrock of effective communication in a relationship. Being an active listener means more than just hearing the words your partner is saying; it is about comprehending their emotions and affording them total attention.

But what does active listening entail? Let's delve deeper into this domain and understand its nuances, practical applications, and the potential it carries to transfigure your romantic relationship.

4.1. The Essence of Active Listening

Active listening is a skill aimed at reaping maximum communication benefits by understanding, interpreting, and responding to the other party. Throughout a conversation, the active listener pays undivided attention to the speaker, refrains from interrupting, and provides feedback only when appropriate.

By acknowledging the speaker's sentiment, active listeners convey empathy and respect, thus fostering a supportive ambiance for dialogue. Such an environment lends itself to more effective conflict resolution and better mutual understanding, boosting the overall quality of the relationship.

4.2. Components of Active Listening

Active listening comprises four primary elements: paraphrasing, clarified understanding, cognitive feedback, and emotional response.

1. *Paraphrasing*: Reframing the speaker's word in your terms validates your understanding and assures them of your engagement.

2. *Clarified Understanding*: Ensuring that your interpretation matches the speaker's intent is crucial. Clarifying questions or statements can prove constructive towards that end.

3. *Cognitive Feedback*: Conveying the impact of the speaker's words helps them understand the consequences and emotional undertone of their comments or actions.

4. *Emotional Response*: This element touches on reacting appropriately to the emotions underlying the conversation.

4.3. Active Listening Versus Passive Listening

The distinction between active and passive listening can be as broad as the difference between night and day. Active listeners take part in the discussion by responding and asking questions when needed, while passive listeners treat conversations like monologues and merely "hear" what's being said. Through active listening, you force yourself to understand and empathize with your partner, leading to harmony and warmth in your relationship. On the contrary, passive listening can often exacerbate misunderstandings and drive a wedge between partners.

4.4. The Role of Nonverbal Cues in Active Listening

Body language plays an invaluable role in making active listening truly "active." This includes maintaining eye contact, nodding in agreement, or showing facial expressions in response to the narrative:

1. A direct gaze conveys interest in the conversation and signals respect for the speaker.

2. A nod signifies affirmation and understanding, encouraging the speaker to continue.

3. Appropriate facial expressions provide a mirror to the speaker's emotions, signaling empathy.

4.5. Techniques to Master Active Listening

Mastering active listening boils down to implementing a specific set of tactics right:

1. Put distractions aside and focus on the conversation.

2. Understand the emotions behind words and tailor your body language to signify understanding.

3. Refrain from interrupting when your partner is speaking.

4. Paraphrase what you hear and seek clarification if unsure.

5. Use open-ended questions to encourage further exploration.

6. Provide cognitive feedback.

7. Give emotional responses appropriately.

4.6. Active Listening in Conflict Resolution

Active listening brings about a transformation in the way conflicts are dealt with in a relationship. With the use of active listening, conflicts can morph into opportunities for constructive dialogue and growth. Feeling heard and understood fosters a communicative ambiance, enabling partners to approach disagreements with less resistance and more openness.

4.7. Overcoming Barriers to Active Listening

It's normal to confront obstacles while striving to master the art of active listening. Be it emotional biases or distraction, it's essential to recognize these barriers and work strategically to overcome them. Practice, patience, self-awareness, and occasional professional help can aid in turning these hindrances into stepping stones.

4.8. Active Listening and Empathy

The soul of active listening lies in empathy. By actively listening, you open yourself up to feel what your partner is feeling and understand their viewpoint. This connection, in turn, radiates empathy in your responses, enhancing your emotional bond.

Remember, the skill of active listening takes time and practice to master. So, be patient with yourself, and make sure to celebrate small victories along the way. The positive changes this skill will bring to your relationship are worth the effort. As you fine-tune your abilities to actively listen, you'll notice your relationship deepening and strengthening in unimaginable ways.

Chapter 5. The Impact of Non-Verbal Communication

In a sea of spoken and written words, it's easy to forget that communication isn't just about the things we say; it's also about the things we don't say. Non-verbal communication, a silent form of discourse that employs body language, facial expressions, eye movement, gestures, touch, and even silence itself, offers a wealth of information beyond spoken words. The potent influence of non-verbal cues within relationships is a significant factor we should not underestimate.

5.1. Deciphering Non-Verbal Cues

To navigate the landscape of non-verbal communication, it's essential to understand the cues expressed through body language. Consider your partner's facial expressions, the direction and intensity of their gaze, their body posture, and the space they maintain or invade during conversations. All these cues deliver a message beyond words, which can profoundly influence how we understand each other and, ultimately, how we relate.

For instance, even when the words convey agreement or acceptance, if a person's arms are crossed on their chest, it might signify discomfort or disagreement. The same holds true for facial expressions: a smile might express joy or conceal stress; a frown might show disagreement or concentration. Understanding these cues is a silent dance you and your partner must learn together.

5.2. The Power of Touch

Touch is another eloquent non-verbal communication tool, carrying an emotional weight words sometimes fail to express. In a relationship, touch serves multiple purposes: comfort, intimacy, relaxation, apologizing, and celebration, among others. However, the same touch can be interpreted differently depending on the context, individual predisposition, past experiences, and cultural norms.

For instance, a reassuring hand on the back can be appreciated in a moment of distress, while the same gesture might feel intrusive or controlling in a different scenario. These layers of complexity call for increased awareness, sensitivity, and mutual agreement about touch boundaries in a relationship.

5.3. Feeding Relationships with Proximity

Proximity - or the physical distance we maintain with others - speaks volumes about our relationships. Couples that are comfortable with each other will usually keep less distance in common settings and might even demonstrate a favor for physical contact such as holding hands or shoulder nudging during shared activities. The act of breaching personal space is typically an expression of trust and deep connection, yet it's crucial to maintain a balance that respects individual autonomy and personal comfort levels.

5.4. Reading the Eyes

Eyes reveal our emotional state, focus, and a depth of feeling words seldom can match. When eyes stray during a conversation, it can indicate distraction, disinterest, or discomfort, yet sustained eye contact often signifies genuine interest and connection. Prolonged eye contact during conflicts can sometimes exacerbate the feeling of hostility, emphasizing the need for sensitivity while interpreting eye communication.

5.5. Cracking the Code of Posture

One's posture is a tell-tale sign of their emotional state and intent. Leaning forward denotes engagement and interest while leaning backward might highlight discomfort or reticence. In face-to-face conversations, mismatched postures can lead to miscommunications. Ensuring your body language aligns with your spoken words and emotional state can help prevent such misunderstandings.

5.6. Cultivating Silent Understanding

While the idea of understanding, interpreting, and effectively using non-verbal cues in a relationship might seem daunting, it is very much achievable. Practice conscious observation, cultivate empathy, and encourage open dialogue about perceptions. Over time, this fosters a silent understanding that strengthens the fabric of your relationship.

5.7. Responsive Non-Verbal Communication

Just as words solicit responses, non-verbal gestures also call for reactions. A smile invites a smile, a frown often brings concern or inquiry, and a withdrawn posture might provoke questions. These reactions fulfill our inherent social cues, promoting a deeper understanding of each other's thoughts and feelings.

5.8. Conclusion

In an ocean of relationships, the most enduring ones are those that sail swiftly in the calm and brave the storm. It is not just words but the inexpressible that helps us understand each other better and harbor a deeper connection. Thus, non-verbal communication, in its many spoken and unspoken dialects, plays a major role in building, strengthening, and preserving the foundation of relationship communication.

Learning to see and hear beyond words is a skill that requires patience and practice. It's not about becoming a master of reading facial expressions or interpreting body language to perfection, but about becoming more attuned to the silent symphony that plays alongside our verbal interactions. A nod, a smile, a look, an embrace - when done with understanding, these silent words can often say more than spoken sentences ever could.

In the end, every relationship is its unique language, created from a mixture of spoken words, silent expressions, shared experiences, and understood meanings. Deciphering this language is a journey of discovery, with the destination being a place of mutual understanding, respect, and lasting love. And remember, while words may bridge minds, it is often the unspoken that bridges hearts.

Chapter 6. Harnessing the Power of Positive Affirmations

Positive affirmations are a powerful tool that can significantly improve communication within couple relationships. With the correct application, these affirmations do not only ensure an uplifting conversation but also fortify the overall bond between partners by forging a more profound sense of understanding and mutual respect.

6.1. The Foundation of Positive Affirmations

Positive affirmations are essentially positive phrases or statements utilized to challenge and combat negative or self-sabotaging thoughts. Often used in self-help and personal development realms, they can be equally effective in strengthening relationships, especially between couples. Not to be confused with pithy platitudes or hollow words, these are constructive affirmations that are backed by genuine feelings or emotions meant to enhance your relational dynamic.

Regular use of positive affirmations contributes to healthier conversations, fosters better understanding, and aids in personal growth. When partners indulge in positive affirmations, they provide a safe space for each other where open, honest, and positive dialogue can take place. This creates an environment of mutual respect and affirmation, where each partner acknowledges and values the other for who they are.

6.2. Positive Affirmation Framework

The creation and use of positive affirmations involve some key steps. For effective outcomes, it is essential to follow this framework.

1. Reflect and understand your current assumptions, beliefs, and feelings.

2. Identify areas where you and your partner could benefit from more positivity.

3. Construct positive affirmations that address these specific areas.

4. Regularly share these affirmations with each other.

Remember, topical affirmations have a better impact as they directly address the issue at hand while promoting positivity.

6.3. Crafting Effective Affirmations

The art of crafting effective affirmations requires practice and understanding. Every affirmation should be personal, actionable, and present-tense.

1. **Personal**: Your affirmations should be aimed specifically at your relationship and tailored to your unique circumstances and needs. For example, if trust is something you want to bolster, an affirmation could be "I trust my partner's choices and decisions."

2. **Actionable**: Your affirmation should inspire action. Good intent is not enough; you need to follow through with actions that reflect the affirmation. Referring to the previous point, this would involve showing faith in your partner's decisions.

3. **Present-Tense**: Scribe your affirmations in a present-tense format, as if they are occurring now. This small linguistic trick has a profound psychological effect. It nurtures a sense of

immediacy and makes the affirmation feel more genuine.

6.4. Implementing Regular Positive Dialogue

Once you've created your affirmative statements, the next task is to incorporate them into your everyday conversations. Be mindful of the situations where they can be introduced organically. Start with just a single affirmation a day and gradually build on it as you become more comfortable and proficient with the practice.

Remember, the key is to make these statements in a conscious and meaningful way that promotes a better connection with your partner. Be authentic and allow your emotions to flow into the exchange. This allows your partner to better receive the affirmation and contributes to a deeper understanding between both of you.

6.5. Dealing with Resistance

You may face resistance while practicing this transformative method of communication, either from yourself or your partner. However, it's crucial to stay patient and persistent. The benefits, though gradual, are substantial, leading to lasting improvements in the relationship.

Don't be disheartened if the change doesn't come overnight. It's essential to give yourself and your partner the space to adjust and adapt to this new form of dialogue. Show kindness, patience, and understanding towards each other.

6.6. Positive Affirmations and Conflict Resolution

Positive affirmations can also be a powerful tool in resolving conflicts. They create a space for constructive dialogue that focuses on solutions rather than problems. Basing your discussions on positivity and love can help to diffuse tense exchanges and promote understanding from both parties.

An affirmation such as "I understand and respect your point of view" can go a long way in managing disagreements. Even in the face of disagreements, this approach ensures that respect and understanding underline the discourse which helps maintain a healthy relationship dynamic.

6.7. Creating an Affirmation Practice

Creating a consistent affirmation practice aids the ease of use, increases frequency, and enhances the overall effectiveness of the exercise. Set a space, a time of day, or perhaps a triggering event, post which both of you can share an affirmation. You could do this over your daily cup of coffee in the morning or just before bed. In time, this will grow to become a seamless part of your relationship routine, strengthening your bond and fostering a healthy communication environment.

Positive affirmations, albeit simple in theory, carry the potential to break the cycle of negative communication and foster an atmosphere of mutual respect, understanding, and love. Building these into your communication repertoire could very well prove to be turning points in improving your relationship dynamics. Other aspects like love, respect, and understanding will likely follow when you radiate positivity in your words and actions. So, seize your power to craft a loving, respectful, and fulfilling relationship. After all, as famed life coach Zig Ziglar once said, "Positive thinking will let you do everything better than negative thinking will."

Chapter 7. Conflict Resolution: From Clashing to Constructive Conversations

Conflict is an inevitable part of any relationship. However, rather than seeing it as an obstacle, it can be viewed as a crucial opportunity for growth, understanding, and increased intimacy. This chapter will guide you through strategies and tactics to transform your clashing conversations into constructive dialogues that strengthen your bond.

7.1. Understanding Conflict

Before diving into conflict resolution, it's essential to understand what conflict really is. Conflict arises when there is a difference in needs, values, interests or desires among people. In a relationship, such differences can be as trivial as choosing a restaurant for dinner or as significant as deciding whether to have children or not.

Remember, conflict itself is not negative; it's the handling of conflict that can either enhance a relationship or lead to its downfall. It's also important to keep in mind that each person's perspective is valid in a disagreement. An empathic perspective, where you try to understand your partner's feelings and viewpoints, can be a powerful foundation for constructive conversations.

7.2. The Role of Effective Communication in Conflict Resolution

Effective communication is the cornerstone of resolving conflicts. It allows both parties to express their feelings and thoughts openly and honestly, promoting understanding and fostering emotional intimacy. Here are some key components of effective communication:

1. Active Listening: Active listening is a skill that requires full attention to the person speaking. It is about hearing the emotions behind the words and understanding the message from the speaker's perspective.

2. Nonverbal Communication: Your body language, tone of voice, and facial expressions often speak louder than words. Ensure your nonverbal cues match your spoken words to avoid miscommunication.

3. Assertive (Not Aggressive) Communication: Being assertive entails expressing your thoughts and feelings clearly and respectfully, without resorting to criticism or defensiveness.

4. Using "I" Statements: Frame your feelings with "I" statements rather than "You" statements. This approach keeps the focus on your feelings and avoids blaming your partner.

7.3. Navigating Through Difficult Conversations

Difficult conversations are a part of any sustainable relationship. It is unnecessary and unhealthy to avoid them. Instead, learn how to navigate through these discussions productively. Here's how:

1. Find the Right Time: Choose a time when you both are calm and open to discussion. Avoid starting a difficult conversation in the heat of anger or frustration.

2. Use a Soft Start-Up: Begin the conversation gently, avoiding blame or criticism. This approach is more likely to elicit a positive response from your partner.

3. Stay Focused: Stay on the topic at hand and resist the urge to

bring up past conflicts or issues.

4. Practice Patience and Respect: Allow your partner to express their thoughts fully before you respond. Respect their feelings and validate their perspective.

7.4. Practical Conflict Resolution Strategies

While every conflict is unique, some handy strategies can work in most situations. Below, we outline some of these strategies:

1. Recognize and Respond to Emotional Bids: Emotional bids are attempts by your partner to connect with you. Recognize these bids and respond to them positively.

2. De-escalate the Argument: When the argument starts to intensify, take a step back to calm down and de-escalate the situation. This break can provide you both with a better perspective and a chance to respond more thoughtfully.

3. Seek First to Understand, Then to be Understood: As Stephen Covey outlined in his 7 Habits of Highly Effective People, this habit can be transformational in conflict resolution.

4. Use Repair Attempts: Repair attempts are efforts to deescalate tension during a disagreement. These can be expressions of affection, humor, or requesting a break.

5. Compromise: Find a middle ground that respects both your needs and your partner's needs.

In the end, remember that effective conflict resolution is a skill that can be learned and practiced. It requires patience, empathy, and above all, the desire to understand your partner's feelings and needs fully. Through constructive conversations, couples can navigate through disagreements, strengthening their relationship's foundation of mutual respect and understanding. It is, indeed, a journey from clashing to constructive conversations.

Chapter 8. Tips to Enhance Openness and Honesty

Openness and honesty are two crucial elements that have the potential to make or break a relationship. It's the lack or abundance of these elements that most often determines the level of satisfaction couples find in their relationship. Indeed, practicing honesty and openness in your relationship is akin to watering a plant, providing it with the necessary nutrients she needs to grow.

First, let's spend some time understanding these fundamental cornerstones of any thriving relationship.

8.1. Understanding Openness and Honesty

Openness is about being willing to share your thoughts, experiences, and feelings with your partner. It's about allowing vulnerability, not feeling the need to censor yourself, and being free and comfortable to communicate anything, no matter how small or large.

Honesty, on the other hand, refers to the act of being truthful and sincere in your words and actions. Honesty means refraining from lying, cheating, or deceiving in any way. It is about being real with your partner both about positive and negative aspects.

8.2. The Importance of Openness and Honesty

In a relationship, honesty and openness foster trust and intimacy - two elements crucial to a strong and healthy relationship. Being open and honest with your partner creates a bond of trust - a reassurance that you can rely on, believe in, and feel secure with your partner.

It's essential to understand that the absence of honesty and openness can lead to confusion, misunderstandings, and conflicts. A lack of transparency and dishonesty can erode trust and break the very foundation of the relationship, leading to unsalvageable damage.

With this understanding at hand, here are some strategies to supplement and enhance openness and honesty in your relationship.

8.3. Create a Safe Space

Creating a safe space for dialogue is step one. It's about ensuring the setting is conducive for open and honest communication. Make sure the space you converse in is free from distractions, adversarial sentiments, and prejudiced conclusions.

Ensure your partner feels secure in expressing their thoughts and feelings without fear of judgment, ridicule, or retaliation. Be mindful of your body language, your tone of voice, and your choice of words. Create an atmosphere of acceptance and love where your partner can feel comfortable while sharing their points of view.

8.4. Develop Emotional Intelligence

Developing emotional intelligence is about understanding your own feelings and those of your partner. This involves cultivating empathy, the ability to read and respond to your own and your partner's emotional states.

Try to connect with your partner on an emotional level. Understand and acknowledge their feelings, and express your own openly and honestly. There's immense power in feeling seen, heard, and validated.

8.5. Foster Trust

Building trust means showing your partner they can rely on you. Be consistent in your words and actions. Follow through on promises made and ensure your actions align with your words.

Trust should be regarded as a precious commodity - one that's easy to lose and hard to regain. Therefore, it's essential to take steps to foster and maintain trust within your relationship.

8.6. Encourage Honesty

To encourage honesty, refrain from reacting negatively to your partner's truth. Remember, everyone has their own reality and experiences. Be respectful of your partner's opinions and experiences.

Avoid responding with anger or dismay when they openly express their thoughts and feelings. Instead, acknowledge their honesty and show gratitude for their trust in you.

8.7. Be Patient

Improving honesty and openness in a relationship is a gradual process. It's important to remember that change doesn't occur overnight. Both you and your partner are likely carrying emotional baggage and past experiences that may hinder open communication.

Patience is key. Celebrate the small victories and continue encouraging each other as you work to establish new habits of open and honest communication.

8.8. Use "I" Statements

Using "I" statements is an effective communication tool to express your feelings without attacking or accusing the other person. Instead of saying, "You make me feel ignored," say, "I feel ignored when you do not respond to my messages." This slight change in communication can create less confrontation and more understanding, encouraging further open and honest dialogue.

Implementing these strategies consistently can bring about a transformational shift in your relationship, helping you foster a strong, deep, and trustworthy bond where openness and honesty thread through every conversation, knitting you closer with every shared word.

Remember, the ultimate key to enhancing openness and honesty lies in your hands. As with every good thing in life, it requires effort, but the rewards of vital, vibrant, and honest communication are well worth it. In the spirit of the wisdom offered in this chapter, take it to heart. Start making changes today for a healthier, happier relationship. Embrace openness, honesty, and enjoy the fruits of a thriving relationship.

Chapter 9. Cultivating Compassion through Conversations

The art of nurturing compassion in conversations is a powerful tool. Its ability to assist you in viewing the world through your partner's eyes not only deepens your understanding, but it can also significantly impact your relationship in a positive way. This chapter aims to help in cultivating compassion through your dialogues, engendering a nurturing and supportive relationship environment.

9.1. Understanding What Compassion Means

Compassion is more than feeling empathy or sympathy towards your partner. It encompasses a desire to undertake measures that alleviate another's struggle. Drenched in understanding and kindness, compassion implies the capacity to sit with discomfort, acknowledging the other person's suffering, emotions, or quandaries, and working together to overcome them.

Professional studies assert that compassionate listening and speaking can yield miracles in relationships, often unraveling an impasse, fostering forgiveness, or creating a deeper connection. It's a powerful act that can infuse relationships with warmth, understanding, and intimacy.

9.2. The Neuroscience of Compassion

Recent research in neuroscience has shed light on how compassion works in our brains. When we feel compassion, our heart rate decreases and our body releases the "bonding hormone" oxytocin, activating regions in the brain linked to empathy, caring, and pleasure. This biological response can lead to a more profound emotional connection with your partner.

It's interesting to note that compassion is like a muscle that you can strengthen with practice. The more we exercise compassion, the stronger it becomes, and the easier it is to employ it during conversations. By consciously incorporating it into our dialogues with our partners, we can cultivate a deep-rooted compassion for and with them.

9.3. Incorporating Compassion into Conversations

To instill compassion in your dialogues, it is crucial first to understand your communication patterns. Pay attention to the tone, words, non-verbal cues, and emotions that are a part of your discussions.

Using "I" statements is an essential part of compassionate communication. It focuses on your feelings and thoughts rather than putting the blame on your partner. For instance, instead of saying, "You never listen to me," you could say, "I feel unheard when I talk about my day." In this way, you voice your feelings without blaming your partner, opening the door to effective communication.

Additionally, practicing empathetic listening can fundamentally alter the way you communicate. This includes listening with the intent to understand rather than to respond, allowing your partner to express their feelings without interruption or judgment. It demonstrates your willingness to understand their viewpoints.

9.4. Building Compassionate Habits

Consistency in practicing compassionate communication can result in the formation of habits. By continually employing these dialoguing measures, it becomes easier to communicate effectively and compassionately.

Mindfulness meditation is also valuable in fostering compassion. It allows you to become aware of your emotions and reactions, enabling you to respond more compassionately during conversations.

Consider implementing a "compassionate conversation time" in your daily routine. These are designated moments where you both communicate openly and honestly, offering a safe space to express feelings or concerns.

9.5. Cultivating Compassion through Conflict

Even the healthiest of relationships experience conflict. During these challenging times, compassion becomes even more crucial. Instead of focusing on winning the argument, shift your focus towards understanding your partner's perspective, feelings, and needs.

The key is to maintain calm and ensure both parties have space to share their points of view. Keep your language gentle and avoid blame or criticism. Remember, conflicts are meant to be resolved, not won.

Navigating through heated emotions might seem overwhelming initially, but with patience, practice, and genuine understanding, it becomes less daunting. Gradually, it strengthens the relationship's foundations, bringing about palpable warmth and security.

Our conversations reflect the dynamics of our relations. A touch of compassion goes a long way in not only understanding our partners but also cherishing them, and embracing their entirety — creating a dialogue that fosters unity and growth. It transforms an everyday conversation into a dialogue of love, empathy, and a deep human connection.

Like all skills, it requires focused effort, continuous practice, and consistent application. However, the fruits of this labour are a profound and lasting connection that transcends the transient trials of coupledom, solidifying it into a lifelong companionship built on understanding, mutual respect, and above all, compassion.

Chapter 10. Building Bonds with Effective Apologies and Forgiveness

Effective apologies and forgiveness are fundamental building blocks for a healthy relationship. They can be seen as the oil that lubricates the intricate machinery of your mutual bond, ensuring its seamless operation despite small mishaps and slight misunderstandings. At this chapter's heart, you will find clear guidance on how to express sincere apologies and forgiveness, two precious tools that can help reconstruct trust, navigate through differences, and ultimately strengthen your bonding.

10.1. Understanding the Philosophy of Apologies

Underpinning each apology is a profound recognition, a humble admittance of a fault or error. This process of admitting our wrongdoing is as humbling as it is crucial for personal growth and maintaining healthy relationships. Apologies open up opportunities for dialogue, provide closure to hurtful incidents, and demonstrate emotional empathy. To misquote a popular adage, nobody is perfect; we all make mistakes. But accepting this imperfection and apologizing when we err sets the stage for individual growth and deeper relationship bonds.

10.2. The Anatomy of an Effective Apology

An effective apology is more than just uttering the words "I'm sorry." It encompasses genuine regret, empathy for the other party's feelings, and a commitment to making amends. Ensuring these elements are present in your apology adds authenticity, enhancing its acceptance and impact.

1. **Acknowledgment**: Recognize the error or the hurt you have caused. Explicitly name what you did wrong. This shows your understanding of the situation as well as your role in it.

2. **Emotion**: Express genuine remorse. The key here isn't about dramatizing your feelings, but communicating sincerely that you feel regretful.

3. **Amends**: Discuss how you plan to make it right. This can involve a change in behavior or another form of restitution.

4. **Future Intent**: Talk about what you will do to ensure this won't happen again. This shows your commitment to learning from mistakes and making positive changes.

10.3. The Power of Forgiveness

While apologies are critical for acknowledging one's mistakes, offering forgiveness is reciprocal — it is a gift that nurtures both the recipient and the one who forgives. It also attests to the strength of your bond and your commitment to moving forward, even when the going gets tough.

1. **Releasing Negativity**: Forgiveness allows you to let go of resentment, anger, and the need for revenge, which only breed negative energy and stress. This release promotes your well-being as well as that of your relationship.

2. **Building Empathy**: Forgiving your partner makes you think about their circumstances, allowing you to understand their point of view and build empathy. This empathic bridge often leads to a more profound connection.

3. **Promoting Growth**: By forgiving, you're signalling your faith in

your partner's ability to change and grow. This affirmation can often be a powerful motivator for positive behavior.

4. **Restoring Trust**: Forgiveness can also serve as a reset button, allowing trust to rebuild and offering a chance to start afresh, albeit wiser and stronger.

10.4. Practical Application: How to Apologize and Offer Forgiveness

Now that you understand the philosophy and benefits of apologies and forgiveness, here are practical ways on how you can apply them in your relationship.

10.4.1. Apology Techniques

1. Maintain eye contact as you offer your apology. This enhances sincerity and indicates your undivided attention.

2. Use "I" statements when admitting your mistake. For instance, say "I messed up" instead of "It was a mistake." This communicates that you take full responsibility.

3. Avoid qualifiers like "but" or "if". They can diminish the impact of your apology as they sound like deflections or excuses.

4. After you've apologized, give your partner time and space to process it. Do not rush them to accept your apology.

10.4.2. Forgiveness Techniques

1. As with an apology, maintain eye contact. This reassures your partner of your earnestness.

2. Verbalize your forgiveness. A simple, "I forgive you" can be incredibly powerful.

3. After forgiving, make an effort not to bring up that particular

mistake in future arguments. Forgiveness means letting go, not filing away for later use.

4. Like with an apology, extend patience and understanding if your partner needs time to make amends.

A journey of a thousand miles begins with a single step. By enhancing your knowledge and embracing and practicing effective apologies and forgiveness, you can take those vital steps towards maintaining a robust, nurturing relationship. This chapter offers the necessary guidance, and the rest is up to you - embrace these tools, and watch your relationship evolve, strengthen, and thrive.

Chapter 11. Maintaining Healthy Communication Habits for Relationship Longevity

Good communication is often lauded as one of the most critical aspects of maintaining a harmonious and enduring relationship. In reality, it's not just about exchanging words but about ensuring those words, whether they be spoken or written, accurately express thoughts, feelings, needs, and desires. While many understand this concept in theory, practical application can sometimes appear arduous. With that in mind, let us delve into the intricacies of maintaining healthy communication habits for the longevity of a relationship.

11.1. Understanding the Basics

Couples often make the mistake of assuming that communication solely centers around talking. Nonetheless, understanding and implementing foundational aspects of communication might be more essential than the talking itself. The pillars of robust, healthy communication are listed below:

- Listening: This goes beyond merely hearing what your partner is saying. Effective listening involves understanding the substance of the discussion and the feelings conveyed. This active listening can transform conversations and ensure that both partners feel heard.

- Non-Verbal Communication: As large as 93% of communication is non-verbal, encompassing elements like body language, tone of voice, and facial expressions. Non-verbal cues reflect directly on the essence of dialogues exchanged.

- Honesty: Honesty should be a default characteristic of any conversation between partners. It is built on a foundation of trust, which is fundamental in any relationship.

- Respect: No conversation should involve disrespect, regardless of the matter being discussed. Respect should be a constant, defining every interaction in your relationship.

11.2. Embracing Vulnerability

Expressing vulnerability and deep emotions can significantly impact the quality of conversations. Many individuals struggle with this point due to discomfort or fear of being hurt. But expressing vulnerability is a sign of strength and is fundamental to open, transparent communication. This openness allows the relationship to deepen, creating a safe haven for both partners to share even their most sensitive thoughts and feelings.

11.3. Dealing with Conflicts

Every relationship will inevitably face conflict - but it's how you handle these conflicts that will dictate their impact on the relationship. Ensure that conflicts are dealt with in a healthy, respectful manner. This means not resorting to insults, judgment, or derogatory remarks. Instead, engage in dialogue that seeks resolution and mutual understanding.

11.4. Balancing Communication

As essential as it is to communicate, finding a balance is crucial since over-communication can easily lead to burnout. It's okay not to share everything, as long as it does not compromise the honesty and transparency within the relationship.

11.5. Developing Empathy

Empathy is the ability to understand and share the feelings of another. It's an integral part of effective communication as it helps you tune into your partner's emotions, fostering a sense of unity and mutual respect. It also translates into being supportive during challenging times.

11.6. Encouraging Positivity

Cultivating an environment that encourages positive expressions is just as crucial as those that allow for disagreement or dismay. Vocalizing love, admiration, and appreciation consistently in the relationship keeps the emotional bank account full.

11.7. Removing Distractions

In an era dominated by digital devices, an often overlooked, but powerful way of improving communication, is by removing distractions. This includes setting aside electronic devices when engaging in significant discussions. Dedicated, uninterrupted time is essential for fruitful communication.

11.8. Regularly Check-Ups

A valuable practice is having regular check-ins with your partner. This can be as simple as setting aside a particular time each week to simply sit down, chat, and touch base.

By understanding and implementing these strategies, couples can navigate the path towards maintaining healthy communication habits for relationship longevity. Remember, open communication is the cornerstone of a strong relationship, and consistent effort in improving that communication will ensure a secure bond for years to come.